Plants that
Eat Animals

By Allan Fowler

Consultant

Janann V. Jenner, Ph.D.

Children's Press®
A Division of Grolier Publishing
New York   London   Hong Kong   Sydney
Danbury, Connecticut

Visit Children's Press® on the Internet at:
http://publishing.grolier.com

Designer: Herman Adler Design Group
Photo Researcher: Caroline Anderson

The photo on the cover shows a fly on the leaf of a Venus's-flytrap.

Library of Congress Cataloging-in-Publication Data

Fowler, Allan.
  Plants that eat animals / by Allan Fowler.
    p. cm. — (Rookie read-about science)
  Includes index.
  Summary: Describes a variety of carnivorous plants, including the
Venus's-flytrap, sundew, pitcher plant, and bladderwort.
    ISBN 0-516-21683-X (lib. bdg.)   0-516-27309-4 (pbk.)
    1. Carnivorous plants—Juvenile literature. [1. Carnivorous plants.]
  I. Title. II. Series.
  QK917.F68   2001
  583'.75—dc21   99-057023

GROLIER
PUBLISHING   1 2 3 4 5 6 7 8 9 10 R 10 09 08 07 06 05 04 03 02 01

All plants need water and minerals to grow. Most plants get them from the soil.

Some plants grow in soil that has few minerals in it. They get food by trapping small animals.

A plant traps a fly.

Venus's-flytrap

The Venus's-flytrap grows
in wetlands in North and
South Carolina. It is about
12 inches tall and has
white flowers. This plant
gets food by trapping
insects.

Each leaf looks like a clam's shell. It has sharp spines around the edges and soft hairs inside.

The leaf gives off a sweet juice that attracts insects.

The sharp leaves of a Venus's-flytrap

When an insect touches
the hairs on a Venus's-
flytrap leaf, the two
halves snap shut.

The plant slowly breaks
down the insect's body
and removes the minerals.

Then the leaf opens
up again.

A Venus's-flytrap traps a cricket.

Sundew plants grow in wet, boggy areas all over the world.

Sundew plant

Each leaf has soft, red
hairs with drops of sticky
liquid on the tips.

When an insect gets stuck
to a few hairs . . .

. . . all the other hairs
on that leaf fold over and
hold the insect in place.

After the plant breaks down the insect's body, the hairs open up again.

The sundew is ready for another meal.

Can you guess how the
pitcher plant got its name?

Its leaves are shaped
like a pitcher and hold
a sweet liquid.

Pitcher plant

When an insect crawls
down into the pitcher,
it gets stuck inside.

It cannot climb back
up the slippery sides.

The insect drowns in
the liquid.

There are many different kinds of pitcher plants.

Trumpet pitcher plant

Purple pitcher plant

Flytrap pitcher plant

Bladderworts live in ponds. Their leaves are covered with tiny bags called bladders.

Bladderworts

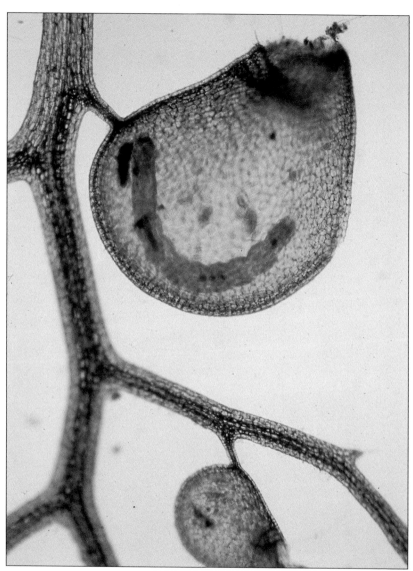

An insect is sucked into a bladder.

If an insect or small
fish touches one of the
bladders, it opens up and
sucks the animal inside.

You probably know many
animals that eat plants.

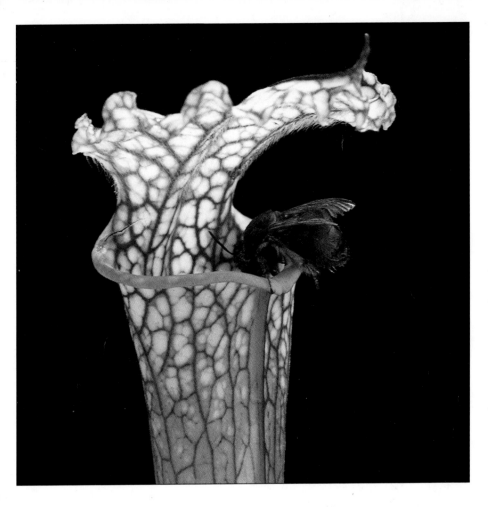

Now you know some
plants that eat animals!

Words You Know

bladderwort

insect

leaf

pitcher plant

30

sundew plant   Venus's-flytrap

Index

About the Author

Allan Fowler is a freelance writer with a background in advertising. Born in New York, he now lives in Chicago and enjoys traveling.

Photo Credits

Photographs ©: Dembinsky Photo Assoc.: 12, 31 left (E. R. Degginger), 20, 22, 23 bottom (Bill Lea), cover, 5 (Gary Meszaros); Peter Arnold Inc.: 13 (Walter H. Hodge), 16 (Matt Meadows), 9, 30 bottom left (Ed Reschke), 29 (Michel Viard); Photo Researchers: 14, 15, 26, 30 top right (Nuridsany et Pérennou), 25, 30 top left (Bob Gibbons/Holt Studios International), 6, 31 right (Gilbert S. Grant) 11 (Dan Suzio); Superstock, Inc.: 3; Tony Stone Images: 28 (Keren Su); Visuals Unlimited: 19, 23 top, 30 bottom right (David Sieren).

ｓ